NEVER GIVE UP

No Matter What

Written by Mason Hagner

Illustrated by Oliver Kryzz Bundoc

This book is dedicated to my dad
because he always says to
NEVER GIVE UP!

One day I asked my dad
if he would play catch with me
with the football.

He said, "Of course!"
with a big smile.

While we played catch,
we talked,
listened to music,
and laughed.

It was so much fun.

After we got done playing catch,
my dad asked me,
"Have you ever thought about
playing football for a team?"

I said, "That sounds like fun!
Let me think about it first."

I really thought about it
and I decided that I wanted
to join a football team.

So, my dad signed me up
and I was really excited
for my first practice!

I went to my first football
practice and we had a blast.

I did high knees on the ladder.

We also learned how to
catch and throw the football.

At the end of practice, we raced each other.

My first practice was a lot of hard work
but it was so exciting.

I couldn't wait for my first game.

Before we started
tackle season, we got
to learn the game by playing
flag football for 6 weeks.

I got to play a lot in every game.

I got 2 touchdowns,
3 extra points,
1 interception,
2 rejections,
and our team got 3rd place medals.

The season was so awesome and I had so much fun!

I couldn't wait for tackle season to start!

After flag football season was over,
we got fitted for tackle
football season.

We had to be measured for
shoulder pads,
helmets,
football pants,
and jerseys.

I even got to pick my own number.

Tackle football season
started with a very tough
3-hour football camp
in the hundred-degree heat.

There were about 250 other kids
at football camp.

We got to do a lot of fun drills like
the ladder,
tackling tubes,
passing drills,
and running through cones.

We even got to play tug of war.

It was so hot and it was really hard work, but I loved it.

After football camp
ended, our team started our
practice season.

It was really hard work.

We had practice three times a week
for two hours every practice.

We practiced in full pads
(helmet, shoulder pads, padded pants,
and cleats) in the really hot weather.

We did several really tough drills and
learned so much about football every practice.

I was very sweaty and very tired.

Football was hard work, but I didn't give up.

After a few weeks
of practice,
we had our first game.

I was really nervous
because I had never played in
an actual tackle football game.

The game was fun but it was also
really tough and a lot hard work.

I almost made an interception
and even made a few tackles.

Sadly, we lost our first game.

I was sad about losing but I still had fun.

Football is hard work but I tried my best and didn't quit.

The next four football games
got even harder and tougher.

I was working really hard at practice
2 to 3 times per week.

It was really hard work.

I was super tired after practice.

As my team played more games,
I got less and less playing time
during games.

I stood on the sidelines
pretty much the whole game and watched
my friends play on the football field.

This made me sad and mad
to watch my friends play but not me.

Football was hard work but I wasn't going to quit.

As practices went on and on,
it got harder and harder
every single time.

I got frustrated working so hard
and not being able to play in the games.

I got so frustrated working so
hard and not being able to play.

The thought of quitting
sounded better than
continuing to work so hard
without playing in the games.

But I also remembered
how important it was
to finish what I started.

Another month went
by and the season was
coming to an end.

One day I told my dad how sad
and frustrated I was. I told him
I was working so hard and wasn't
getting a chance to play in the games.

My dad always taught me
to never quit no matter what.

My dad gave me a choice. He said, "You can
quit now if you really want to or you can decide
to keep going and finish what you started."

I decided to keep going and finish what I started,
because I didn't want to quit. I wanted to have a chance
to possibly play in the last game.

Football was hard but I didn't quit.

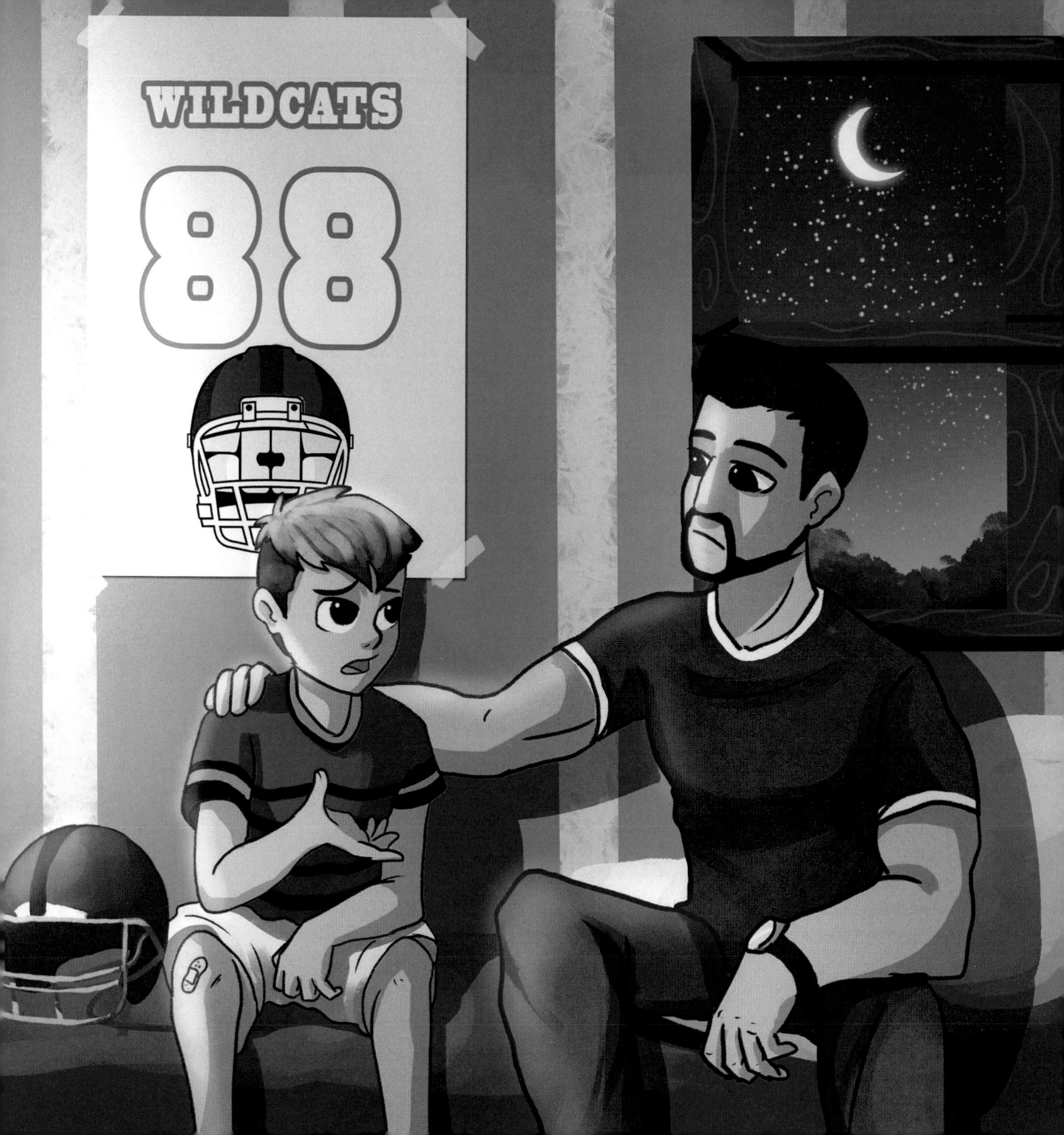
WILDCATS
88

After months of practices
and 7 full season games,
the last game of the season
was here.

I went to the game hoping
I was going to play.

I am happy to say my wish came true.
I got to play more than half the game.

I made a few tackles, I got the ball a few times,
and one of my other teammates got a touchdown
because I blocked for him.

Football was hard work and there were times
I felt like quitting, but I never did.

I'm so glad I never quit.

I wanted to write this book
and dedicate it to anyone
who is thinking about quitting
something they have started.

Sometimes we think quitting is the
easiest way out of something.

We often think of quitting
when things get tough or don't go our way.

You never know what good things could happen
if you just stick with it and NEVER GIVE UP.

You got this!
NEVER QUIT!

Made in the USA
Las Vegas, NV
23 October 2020